HEALING JOURNAL

by

Cynthia Owen

Healing Journal
ISBN: 978-0-9971652-0-3
Copyright © 2016 by Cynthia Owen

All rights reserved. No part of this book may be reproduced in any form without permission in writing from the publisher, except in the case of brief quotations embodied in critical articles or reviews.

All Scripture quotations are from the King James Version of the Bible.

Published by:
JC Owen and Associates, Inc.
3558 Round Barn Blvd., Suite 200
Santa Rosa, CA 95403

Printed in the United States of America.

Dear Friend,

The healing journal was created to help you believe God for your healing. Healing can sometimes come to our lives right away, or at other times it can be a process for us to be healed.

My heart's desire is to help you turn your spirit, mind, and body to the one who created you, and who is your healer, Jesus Christ.

I'm convinced that God is always trying to help us understand healing, but sometimes we just don't find ourselves in faith or understanding about how healing works or how we receive healing in our own life and bodies.

Often when we don't feel well, or our circumstances are screaming defeat, it's easy to lose hope and to question just where God is in the middle of our tough times.

We can question ourselves and God at the same time. We can be overtaken by fear, loneliness, and discouragement. We are often looking for answers and direction for our healing.

Each day as you write in your journal you will get a glimpse of what God has to say about healing.

My husband and I have prayed for the sick for many years now, and we have learned about, and seen God do, many miracles. God has also taught us some of His truths about how to receive healing. On the next page I have listed some of these truths to help you.

Be healed in the name of Jesus!

Cindy

KEYS FOR YOUR HEALING

Hebrews 11:6 says, "But without faith it is impossible to please him: for he that cometh to God must believe that he is, and that he is a rewarder of them that diligently seek him."

Be fully persuaded in your mind that God truly wants to heal *you*. It's one thing to know that God heals, but it's quite another to know that God wants to heal *you*.

Have a very strong prayer life. Read the word of God as often as you can daily. If you are too weak to read for yourself, then have someone get you the bible on CD so you can listen to it everyday.

Memorize the scriptures that are written regarding healing. Memorize, believe and confess them aloud throughout the day.

Get rid of all negative confession, and ONLY speak the word of God regarding your health and healing.

Call those things that are not as though they are (Romans 4:17).

Constantly thank God for your healing.

Have those around you pray for you.

Go to the elders of your church and be anointed with oil.

Eat as healthy as possible.

Believe God according to His Word!

Never give up!

Since Jesus said He is your healer, *take Him at His Word!*

HEALING

"Who his own self bare our sins in his own body on the tree, that we, being dead to sins, should live unto righteousness: by whose stripes ye were healed."
1 Peter 2:24

Insights:
_____
_____
_____
_____
_____
_____
_____
_____
_____
_____
_____
_____
_____
_____
_____
_____
_____

Healing

My Declaration: *"Lord, I thank you for bearing all of my sins in your body on the cross, so that by faith I am dead to sins and alive to righteousness, and by your stripes **I am healed!**"*

HEALING

"For we walk by faith, not by sight."
2 Corinthians 5:7

Insights:

Healing

My Declaration: *"Lord, I declare that I will not walk by sight. I make the choice to walk by faith in the promises of your word.* **I believe in your promises** *that you have given to me regarding my healing."*

HEALING

*"My tongue shall speak of thy word:
for all thy commandments are righteousness."
Psalm 119:172*

Insights:

Healing

My Declaration: *"Lord, I declare that the confession of my mouth will not be negative. I will put a watch over my mouth, and my tongue will only speak of the blessings that **you have promised me regarding my healing**."*

HEALING

*"With long life will I satisfy him,
and shew him my salvation."
Psalm 91:16*

Insights:
_____
_____
_____
_____
_____
_____
_____
_____
_____
_____
_____
_____
_____
_____
_____
_____
_____
_____
_____
_____

Healing

My Declaration: *"Lord, I declare that I will have a life that is **full of satisfaction and joy**, and that all of the desires of my heart **will be fulfilled in my lifetime**."*

HEALING

"So then faith cometh by hearing, and hearing by the word of God."
Romans 10:17

Insights:

Healing

My Declaration: *"Lord, I declare that, as I hear your word, faith is actually coming to me. Your word will change my circumstances, and as I continue to hear and confess your word,* **I know I can count on your healing.**"

HEALING

*"Who by him do believe in God, that raised him
up from the dead, and gave him glory;
that your faith and hope might be in God."*
1 Peter 1:21

Insights:

Healing

My Declaration: *"Lord, I declare that my faith and hope are in you alone. You have shown me that you have the ability to raise the dead. Therefore, I will call those things in my life that are not yet **as though they are complete**."*

HEALING

*"This is my comfort in my affliction:
for thy word hath quickened me."
Psalm 119:50*

Insights:

Healing

My Declaration: *"Lord, I declare that your word comforts me in all afflictions. Lord, I believe that **your word is quickening me as I pray** this declaration."*

HEALING

"And Jesus said unto him, Go thy way; thy faith hath made thee whole. And immediately he received his sight, and followed Jesus in the way."
Mark 10:52

Insights:

Healing

My Declaration: *"Lord, I declare that I have enough faith to be made whole. As I go, I can expect to be immediately healed. I don't have to wait for months for **my healing**."*

HEALING

"But what saith it? The word is nigh thee, even in thy mouth, and in thy heart: that is, the word of faith, which we preach."
Romans 10:8

Insights:
_____
_____
_____
_____
_____
_____
_____
_____
_____
_____
_____
_____
_____
_____
_____
_____
_____
_____
_____

Healing

My Declaration: *"Lord, I declare that your word is strong in my heart, and the confession of your word is in my mouth. Your words of faith **make me whole**."*

HEALING

"That your faith should not stand in the wisdom of men, but in the power of God."
1 Corinthians 2:5

Insights:

Healing

My Declaration: *"Lord, I declare that I will not stand with my faith in the wisdom of men, but I will put my faith in **your power, which is working mightily in me.**"*

HEALING

"And he healed many that were sick of divers diseases, and cast out many devils; and suffered not the devils to speak, because they knew him."
Mark 1:34

Insights:
_____
_____
_____
_____
_____
_____
_____
_____
_____
_____
_____
_____
_____
_____
_____

Healing

My Declaration: "Lord, I declare that you have authority over all sickness and disease. You have the absolute power to cast out all devils, **and to set anyone who is captive free**."

HEALING

"But he was wounded for our transgressions, he was bruised for our iniquities: the chastisement of our peace was upon him; and with his stripes we are healed."
Isaiah 53:5

Insights:

_____
_____
_____
_____
_____
_____
_____
_____
_____
_____
_____
_____
_____
_____
_____
_____

Healing

My Declaration: *"Lord, I declare that I do not have to carry life's burdens because you have borne all of my weaknesses, sicknesses and pains. Because of the stripes you took, I can live in peace. **I am healed!**"*

HEALING

"And straightway the fountain of her blood was dried up; and she felt in her body that she was healed of that plague."
Mark 5:29

Insights:

_____
_____
_____
_____
_____
_____
_____
_____
_____
_____
_____
_____
_____
_____
_____
_____
_____

Healing

My Declaration: *"Lord, I declare that I feel your healing power at work in my body. I can sense your healing power. You are the creator of my body and **your word has the ability to heal me.**"*

HEALING

"And they cast out many devils, and anointed with oil many that were sick, and healed them."
Mark 6:13

Insights:

_____
_____
_____
_____
_____
_____
_____
_____
_____
_____
_____
_____
_____
_____
_____
_____
_____
_____
_____
_____

Healing

My Declaration: *"Lord, I declare that you have the power to heal me. I can feel your healing power at work in my body. **Your word has the ability to heal me.**"*

HEALING

"Thy word is a lamp unto my feet, and a light unto my path."
Psalm 119:105

Insights:
_____
_____
_____
_____
_____
_____
_____
_____
_____
_____
_____
_____
_____
_____
_____
_____
_____
_____
_____

Healing

My Declaration: *"Lord, I declare that your word is a light that continues to show me the path in which I should walk. Your word guides me everyday. I have confidence in your word and **in its ability to guide me.**"*

HEALING

"But so much the more went there a fame abroad of him: and great multitudes came together to hear, and to be healed by him of their infirmities."
Luke 5:15

Insights:

Healing

My Declaration: *"Lord, I declare that, as I position myself around your anointing, your power has the ability to **bring healing into my life.** I will continue to place my life in places where I can hear the word of God."*

HEALING

"And they brought unto him all sick people that were taken with divers diseases and torments, and those which were possessed with devils, and those which were lunatic, and those that had the palsy; and he healed them."
Matthew 4:24

Insights:

_____
_____
_____
_____
_____
_____
_____
_____
_____
_____
_____
_____
_____
_____
_____

Healing

My Declaration: *"Lord, I declare that not one problem is too big for you to heal.* **You have given me** *many examples of your ability to heal all diverse types of diseases. I feel your healing power* **at work in my body.** *I can sense your healing power."*

HEALING

"And the whole multitude sought to touch him: for there went virtue out of him, and healed them all."
Luke 6:19

Insights:

_____
_____
_____
_____
_____
_____
_____
_____
_____
_____
_____
_____
_____
_____
_____
_____
_____
_____

Healing

My Declaration: *"Lord, I declare that I will pursue a touch from you. You have virtue that flows to your children. You have given me confidence that **you have the ability and the desire to heal everyone who seeks you for healing**."*

HEALING

"Now when the sun was setting, all they that had any sick with divers diseases brought them unto him; and he laid his hands on every one of them, and healed them."
Luke 4:40

Insights:

Healing

My Declaration: *"Lord, I declare that I feel your healing power at work in my body. I can sense your healing power. You are the creator of my body and **your word has the ability to heal me**."*

HEALING

*"I am afflicted very much: quicken me,
O Lord, according unto thy word."
Psalm 119:107*

Insights:

Healing

My Declaration: *"Lord, I declare that your word has the ability to quicken my mortal body. Although affliction may be present,* ***your word has all power and authority over affliction.****"*

HEALING

"For unclean spirits, crying with loud voice, came out of many that were possessed with them: and many taken with palsies, and that were lame, were healed."
Acts 8:7

Insights:

_____
_____
_____
_____
_____
_____
_____
_____
_____
_____
_____
_____
_____
_____
_____

Healing

My Declaration: *"Lord, I declare that I feel your healing power at work in my body. I can sense your healing power. You are the creator of my body and **your word has the ability to heal me**."*

HEALING

"And make straight paths for your feet, lest that which is lame be turned out of the way; but let it rather be healed."
Hebrews 12:13

Insights:

_____
_____
_____
_____
_____
_____
_____
_____
_____
_____
_____
_____
_____
_____
_____
_____
_____
_____

Healing

My Declaration: *"Lord, I declare that I will walk in your straight paths.* ***I choose the paths of healing.*** *I shun sickness and disease.* ***I will give no place in my life*** *for Satan's sickness and disease."*

HEALING

"Confess your faults one to another, and pray one for another, that ye may be healed. The effectual fervent prayer of a righteous man availeth much."
James 5:16

Insights:

_____
_____
_____
_____
_____
_____
_____
_____
_____
_____
_____
_____
_____
_____
_____
_____
_____

Healing

My Declaration: *"Lord, I declare that I will continue to confess my faults so I can be spiritually healed. I will pray heartfelt and continual prayers so that they will be **effective for my healing**."*

HEALING

"For this people's heart is waxed gross, and their ears are dull of hearing, and their eyes they have closed; lest at any time they should see with their eyes, and hear with their ears, and should understand with their heart, and should be converted, and I should heal them."
Matthew 13:15

Insights:

_____
_____
_____
_____
_____
_____
_____
_____
_____
_____
_____
_____
_____
_____
_____

Healing

My Declaration: "*Lord, I declare that I will not allow my heart to become hard. I will be quick to listen to your voice, and my eyes will be focused on the moving of your Holy Spirit.* ***I will follow your instructions all the days of my life.***"

HEALING

"The same heard Paul speak: who stedfastly beholding him, and perceiving that he had faith to be healed, said with a loud voice, Stand upright on thy feet. And he leaped and walked."
Acts 14:9-10

Insights:

_____
_____
_____
_____
_____
_____
_____
_____
_____
_____
_____
_____
_____
_____
_____
_____
_____

Healing

My Declaration: *"Lord, I declare that I feel your healing power at work in my body. I can sense your healing power. You are the creator of my body and **your word has the ability to heal me.**"*

HEALING

"But when Jesus knew it, he withdrew himself from thence: and great multitudes followed him, and he healed them all."
Matthew 12:15

Insights:
_____
_____
_____
_____
_____
_____
_____
_____
_____
_____
_____
_____
_____
_____
_____
_____
_____
_____
_____

Healing

My Declaration: *"Lord, I declare that you know all things. As I follow you, I am confident that, just like you healed **all** who came to you then, **you will heal me of all my diseases now.**"*

HEALING

"Thou art my hiding place and my shield: I hope in thy word."
Psalm 119:114

Insights:
_____
_____
_____
_____
_____
_____
_____
_____
_____
_____
_____
_____
_____
_____
_____
_____
_____
_____
_____
_____
_____

Healing

My Declaration: *"Lord, I declare that you are **my hiding place**. You are **my shield** from the strategies of my enemies. My hope is in you alone. I can be confident that **you will protect me**."*

HEALING

"And Jesus said unto them, Because of your unbelief: for verily I say unto you, If ye have faith as a grain of mustard seed, ye shall say unto this mountain, Remove hence to yonder place; and it shall remove; and nothing shall be impossible unto you."
Matthew 17:20

Insights:
___
___
___
___
___
___
___
___
___
___
___
___
___
___
___
___

Healing

My Declaration: *"Lord, I declare that I will be on guard for unbelief. I seek you only, and position myself around your word. My confession will be the word of God. I will remain watchful and **will not allow my mouth to speak words of unbelief.**"*

HEALING

*"And great multitudes followed him;
and he healed them there."*
Matthew 19:2

Insights:

_____
_____
_____
_____
_____
_____
_____
_____
_____
_____
_____
_____
_____
_____
_____
_____
_____

Healing

My Declaration: "Lord, I declare that, as I follow you, **I will be healed**. You did not turn anyone away who came to you for healing. Your word says that **you healed them all**."

HEALING

*"Heaviness in the heart of man maketh it stoop:
but a good word maketh it glad."*
Proverbs 12:25

Insights:

_____
_____
_____
_____
_____
_____
_____
_____
_____
_____
_____
_____
_____
_____
_____
_____

My Declaration: "*Lord, I declare that I will be on guard not to allow my heart to become heavy so that it brings discouragement to me.* **I will focus on the word of God, because it brings me into joy and gladness.**"

HEALING

"And Jesus went forth, and saw a great multitude, and was moved with compassion toward them, and he healed their sick."
Matthew 14:14

Insights:
_____
_____
_____
_____
_____
_____
_____
_____
_____
_____
_____
_____
_____
_____
_____
_____
_____
_____

Healing

My Declaration: *"Lord, I declare that I feel your healing power at work in my body. I can sense your healing power. You are the creator of my body and **your word has the ability to heal me.**"*

HEALING

"But if the Spirit of him that raised up Jesus from the dead dwell in you, he that raised up Christ from the dead shall also quicken your mortal bodies by his Spirit that dwelleth in you."
Romans 8:11

Insights:

My Declaration: *"Lord, I declare that my confidence is in you alone. Your word is the standard that I will hold when believing the outcome of difficult circumstances in my life.* **I'm counting on your Holy Spirit, who lives in me, to heal my body.**"

HEALING

"Every word of God is pure: he is a shield unto them that put their trust in him."
Proverbs 30:5

Insights:
_____
_____
_____
_____
_____
_____
_____
_____
_____
_____
_____
_____
_____
_____
_____
_____
_____

Healing

My Declaration: "Lord, I declare that I don't have to worry about if your word is true. ***I can be confident*** that you are a shield about me. As I continue to trust you, ***I know you will deliver me.***"

HEALING

"He sent his word, and healed them, and delivered them from their destructions."
Psalm 107:20

Insights:

Healing

My Declaration: *"Lord, I believe that you sent your word and it's coming toward me every second of every day. Therefore, I receive it, I believe it, and that makes me confident that **I'm healed and delivered from all destructions**."*

HEALING

*"Bless the Lord, O my soul, and forget not all his benefits:
Who forgiveth all thine iniquities; who healeth all thy diseases;
Who redeemeth thy life from destruction;"*
Psalm 103:2-4

Insights:
_____
_____
_____
_____
_____
_____
_____
_____
_____
_____
_____
_____
_____
_____

My Declaration: *"Lord, I declare that, according to your word and by the power of your Spirit,* **I am redeemed, my sins have been forgiven, and my body is healed in Jesus' name!"**